P-38 Lightning

Written by David Doyle

In Action®

Squadron Signal® Publications

Line Illustrations by Melinda Turnage

(Front Cover) Dubbed the "forked-tail devil" by Luftwaffe pilots and "two planes, one pilot" by the Japanese, the twin-engine Lockheed P-38 Lightning was the only U.S. fighter aircraft to be in production throughout the U.S. involvement in World War II. The P-38 was used in the European, China-Burma-India, and Pacific Theaters, and was flown by two of America's top aces – Richard Bong, 40 victories; and Thomas McGuire, 38 victories. (National Archives via Stan Piet).

(Back Cover) This F-5E photo-reconnaissance Lightning of the 7th Photographic Reconnaissance Group flew from USAAF Station 234, Mount Farm, Oxfordshire, England, in the final year of World War II. The aircraft is painted in synthetic haze camouflage with invasion stripes under the booms only. The aircraft number, 695, and the fronts of the propeller spinners are white. (Robert Astrella via Stan Piet)

About the In Action® Series

In Action® books, despite the title of the genre, are books that trace the development of a single type of aircraft, armored vehicle, or ship from prototype to the final production variant. Experimental or "one-off" variants can also be included. Our first *In Action®* book was printed in 1971.

ISBN 978-0-89747-849-6

Proudly printed in the U.S.A.
Copyright 2017 Squadron/Signal Publications
1115 Crowley Drive, Carrollton, TX 75006-1312 U.S.A.

Military/Combat Photographs and Snapshots

If you have any photos of aircraft, armor, soldiers, or ships of any nation, particularly wartime snapshots, please share them with us and help make Squadron/Signal's books all the more interesting and complete in the future. Any photograph sent to us will be copied and returned as requested. Electronic images are preferred. The donor will be fully credited for any photos used. Please send them to:

Squadron/Signal Publications
1115 Crowley Drive
Carrollton, TX 75006-1312 U.S.A.
www.Squadron.com

(Title Page) One of the premier fighters of World War II, the Lockheed P-38 Lightning was a sleek, twin-engined aircraft with booms and lethal firepower. Noted for its speed, endurance, and versatility, the Lightning served in virtually all of the U.S. Army's areas of operation and fulfilled a variety of applications, including photo-reconnaissance, ground attack, interception, pathfinding, and night fighting. (Stan Piet collection)

Acknowledgments

This book would not have been possible without the generous assistance of Stan Piet; Tom Kailbourn; Jim Gilmore; Scott Taylor; the staff at the National Archives and Records Administration; the Dyersburg Army Air Force Base Memorial Association; the San Diego Air and Space Museum; and Brett Stolle and the staff at the National Museum of the United States Air Force. I am especially thankful for the help and support of my wife Denise. All photographs not otherwise attributed are from the National Museum of the United States Air Force.

Introduction

Though more than 70 years have passed since the Lockheed P-38's maiden flight, the distinctive shape of the aircraft remains instantly recognizable. This design was the result of the combined efforts of two of America's most notable aircraft designers: Hall Hibbard and Clarence "Kelly" Johnson.

Johnson – whose name is well known in aviation circles for such famed aircraft as the P-80, F-104, U-2, and SR-71 – was Hibbard's assistant in February 1937. That was the year the U.S. Army Air Corps solicited proposals for a new pursuit aircraft – the aircraft that was destined to become the Lightning.

The Lightning would become unique in that it was the only U.S. pursuit-type (P-) aircraft that would remain in continuous production throughout the duration of World War II. This feat is all the more remarkable given not only the rapid advancement in aircraft design during the war years and the evolving U.S. air-power doctrine, but also due to the fact that both the prototype XP-38 and the first service-test (YP-38) aircraft were destroyed in crashes.

The Air Corps needed an aircraft with a top speed of 360 m.p.h. that could climb to 20,000 feet in six minutes. Also required was sufficient fuel capacity to fly at full throttle for one hour. These and other attributes were laid out in "Specification X-608," which the Air Corps distributed to aircraft manufacturers in early 1937. Among the recipients was Lockheed. There Hibbard and Johnson began sketching designs, all of which had two engines, for what would be Lockheed's first pursuit-type aircraft.

Also created to meet Specification X-608 was Bell's XP-39. While in the initial form shown here the aircraft held potential as an interceptor, ultimately the decision to remove the supercharger resulted in an aircraft best suited for ground attack.

The Curtiss P-36 Hawk was a predecessor of the P-38 as a U.S. pursuit aircraft. The prototype first took to the air in May 1935, and deliveries of the standardized P-36A began in April 1938. Several versions were produced, and the aircraft was exported to a number of countries, including Great Britain and France. Obsolete by the beginning of World War II, several Hawks sortied during the Pearl Harbor attack and shot down two Japanese Zeros for the loss of one Hawk.

In early 1937 the Army Air Corps contracted with Curtiss to convert one P-36 to the new turbo-supercharged, liquid-cooled Allison V-1710 engine. The result, the XP-37, had a streamlined cowling and propeller spinner, with the radiators mounted on the sides of the cowl and the cockpit relocated toward the rear of the aircraft. Although the Army ordered 13 test aircraft designated YP-37, the airplane was not adopted for service. The turbo-supercharged V-1710, however, would soon be adapted to the P-38.

3

XP-38

Clarence "Kelly" L. Johnson and his design team at Lockheed began developing the XP-38 in January 1937, and U.S. Army Air Corps issued a contract to Lockheed on 23 June to build one prototype, given the Air Corps serial number 38-326. It was powered by twin turbo-supercharged Allison engines (the V-1710-11 on the left side and the V-1710-15 on the right) and was intended to achieve speeds 100 miles per hour faster than other U.S. pursuit aircraft at that time. Although the XP-38 was similar in appearance to the production P-38, the arrangement of the intakes on the booms was quite different.

The XP-38 made its maiden flight on 27 January 1939. The aircraft was designed with counter-rotating propellers, with the blades rotating inward at the top. This configuration yielded better propeller-torque and handling properties than would have been the case if the propellers rotated in the same direction. The scoop on the bottom of each engine nacelle was an air intake for the oil coolers and was retractable.

The styling now familiar as the P-38 was seen to have many advantages. As expected, its tricycle landing gear eased ground operations, and the center fuselage, its nose free of power plant, allowed for a concentration of weaponry directly ahead of the pilot. Aiming the weapons became merely a matter of pointing the aircraft at the target.

In order to meet the Army requirements for rate of climb as well as top speed, early on Hibbard and Johnson decided that twin engines were a necessity. The twin boom layout ultimately selected by Hibbard and Johnson provided stability, as well as housings for the landing gear and turbosuperchargers, the latter being key to the high-altitude performance of the twin Allison V-1710 twelve-cylinder engines. Adding to the streamlining was the innovative use of butt-jointed, flush-riveted skin.

Impressed with the design, Specification X-608 author Lt. Benjamin Kelsey of Wright Field's Pursuit Projects Office recommended the Air Corps order one of the radical new aircraft for tests. Air Corps Contract 9974, awarded on 23 June 1937, was for one XP-38. This plane, Air Corps serial number 37-457, cost $163,000. One year later, the design work virtually complete, construction of the prototype began in Burbank, California.

As work progressed, Jim Gerschler, project engineer, added the innovation of having contra-rotating engines. In this manner, the torque of the two engines cancelled each other out, eliminating control problems at takeoff and landing.

Teams of skilled Lockheed workers assembled the prototype, which was classified, in secrecy. Once assembled and after passing initial checks, the XP-38 was partially dismantled, shrouded in tarpaulins and, on New Year's Eve 1938, trucked from Burbank to March Field, in then-remote Riverside, California. There, several days were spent reassembling the big fighter, after which ground tests were performed. At that time, Lockheed had no test pilots on its payroll, so Lt. Ben Kelsey of the Pursuit Projects Office served in that capacity. Kelsey, who eventually rose to the rank of Brigadier General, was well-qualified for this additional task, as he had a Master's degree in Engineering from MIT, and was also an experienced test pilot. On 27 January 1939, with Lt. Kelsey at the controls, the XP-38 lifted into the air on its maiden flight.

On 11 February Lt. Kelsey and the XP-38 left March Field on a ferry flight to the Air Corps test center at Wright Field, near Dayton, Ohio. It was also hoped to set a Los Angeles-to-Dayton speed record with the flight. *En route* Kelsey noted that the aircraft was making remarkably good time, arriving in Amarillo for refueling after only 2 hours and 48 minutes. The Amarillo-to-Dayton flight took only 2 hours and 45 minutes, and Kelsey and the XP-38 were met by General Hap Arnold, Chief of the Army Air Corps. After a brief discussion, Arnold and Kelsey decided to refuel and fly on to New York, in an effort to beat Howard Hughes's cross-country speed record. As Kelsey descended to Mitchel Field, Long Island, the carburetor air intakes iced up. The resultant loss of power on landing approach caused the aircraft to come in short of the runway, crashing onto the Cold Stream Golf Course. Kelsey survived, but the XP-38 was destroyed.

However, the design had shown great potential, and on 27 April 1939, the Air Corps ordered 13 service-test aircraft, the "Y" in their YP-38 designation indicating this use.

Twelve of the YP-38 prototypes were used for flight testing, and the remaining one was subjected to extreme stress testing. The final YP-38 was delivered in June 1941. The lack of fillets around the joint between the leading edge of the wing and the central nacelle is evident in this photograph of a YP-38 in flight. Below the wing is the air intake of the turbo-supercharger system. Mass balances have been installed on the elevators. It was believed initially that the mass balances alleviated tail buffeting at high speeds, but design chief Kelly Johnson later divulged that they were not effective. (Air Force Historical Research Agency)

The YP-38, designated "Model 122" by Lockheed, was the next step in the evolution of the P-38. The power plant of the YP-38 differed from that of the XP-38 in significant ways. First, a pair of 1,150 h.p. Allison V-1710-27/-29 (F2R/F2L) engines with B-2 turbo superchargers and spur reduction gearing replaced the V-1710-11 and -15 of the prototype, which had featured epicyclic gearing. This new arrangement caused the engine's thrust line to be raised. Also, the tops of the propellers now rotated outward rather than inward as on the XP-38. This change reduced tail buffeting, but made single-engine operation significantly more challenging. The retractable oil and intercooler intake under each prop spinner was replaced by a pair of cooling intakes.

Large radiator scoops on both sides of each boom would become a characteristic feature on the production P-38.

Development of the aircraft took a year and a half, as Lockheed expanded its Burbank facilities. Then, nearly 17 months after the contract was finalized, Marshall Headle took the first YP-38 into the air on 16 September 1940. The first YP-38 was delivered to the Army in March 1941, and the final YP-38 was completed in June of the same year.

During trials the YP-38s suffered severe tail buffeting at speeds near Mach 0.68, particularly in dives, making pull-out difficult. On 4 November 1941 the tail booms of the first YP-38 came off during a dive, and test pilot Ralph Virden was killed.

While the Army believed that the tail booms had come off as a result of flutter, extensive testing revealed the problem to be compressibility and the shifting of the center of lift as airflow increased.

Nacelle/Boom Development

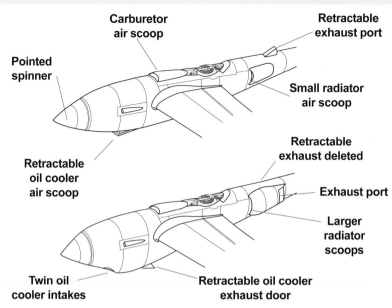

Carburetor air scoop

Retractable exhaust port

Pointed spinner

Small radiator air scoop

Retractable oil cooler air scoop

Retractable exhaust deleted

Exhaust port

Larger radiator scoops

Twin oil cooler intakes

Retractable oil cooler exhaust door

Lockheed test pilot Marshall Headle runs up the engines of the first YP-38, serial number 39-689, in September 1940. The second YP-38 went to Langley Field, Virginia, to serve as a full-sized wind-tunnel test aircraft. The rest of the 13 YP-38s were mostly assigned to the 1st Pursuit Group, Selfridge Field, Michigan.

A test pilot is taking a YP-38 for a flight high above a network of desert washes. Marked in small black numerals on the side of the nose is a small number, either 2262 or 2282. Mass balances, initially not present on YP-38 elevators, have been installed. (Stan Piet collection)

In the common prewar U.S. Army Air Corps markings scheme, the YP-38s were marked "U.S." on the underside of the starboard wing and "Army" on the bottom of the port wing. Below the port engine nacelle is the open oil-cooler shutter. (National Archives)

A number of P-38s near completion on Lockheed's Burbank, California, assembly line in May 1941. Given the date, these probably were among the 29 initial P-38s, the first of which was delivered to the Army Air Corps in June 1941. (Jim Gillmore collection)

As P-38s near completion on the Lockheed assembly line, personnel pause to go over a blueprint. The starboard boom of the closest plane is stenciled with the identification number 3001R, while the port boom is stenciled 3001L. Jacks support the booms. (Jim Gilmore collection)

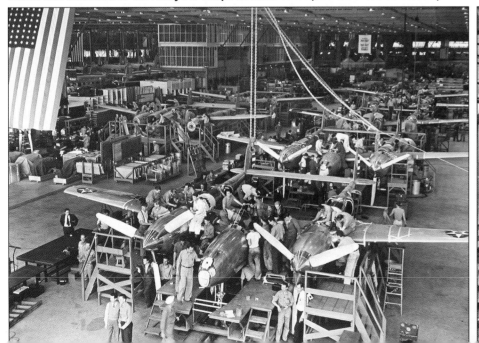

When the YP-38 was in high-speed flight at Mach .67, it had tendencies to experience tail buffeting and assume a nose-down attitude, resulting in a compressibility stall with the controls locking up. The buffeting problem was solved by June 1941 by fitting fillets around the leading edge of the wing where it met the central nacelle. The compressibility problem would take much longer to overcome. Aside from the large air scoop located on top of each boom over the wing and the lack of guns in the nose, this aircraft closely resembled the early-production P-38s. (Air Force Historical Research Agency)

The test pilot is grasping the circular control wheel in this view of the first YP-38. The elevator counterweights were a later addition to the P-38 line. The propellers have cuffs that were later discontinued, and the blades are not painted.

This aircraft is the first YP-38, delivered to the U.S. Army Air Corps in September 1940. The counter-rotating propellers of the YP-38 rotated outward at the top: the reverse of the rotation of the XP-38. The prototype was devoid of markings except for the national insignia and some stencils.

From head on, the YP-38 presents a sleek, streamlined appearance. The cuffs on the propellers have here been discontinued. There were air inlets for the oil coolers on the chin of each engine nacelle, in place of the retractable scoop on the bottom of each nacelle that featured on the XP-38. The YP-38s experienced a change of engine models over the XP-38: now, an Allison V-1710-27 was in the right position and a V-1710-29 in the left.

P-38 Lightning Development

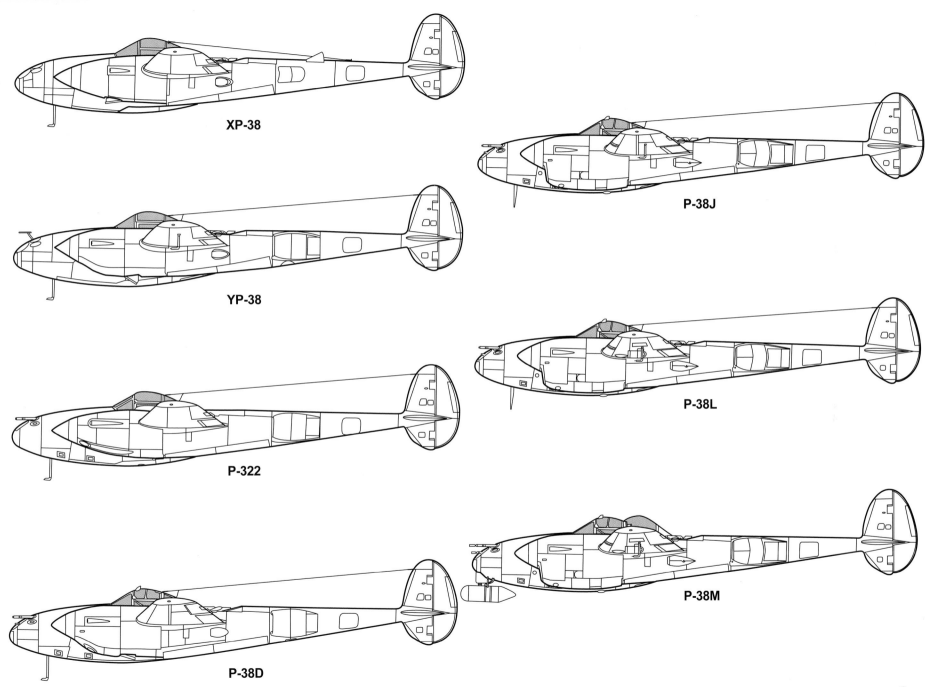

XP-38

YP-38

P-322

P-38D

P-38J

P-38L

P-38M

The P-38 was similar in design to the YP-38, with some improvements, including the addition of armor for the pilot. Most P-38s underwent operational evaluation with the 1st Pursuit Group at Selfridge Field, Michigan. Shown here is the first P-38, USAAF serial number 40-744, which translated to the tail number 0744, the zero standing for the last digit of the fiscal year in which the aircraft was ordered, 1940. A light-colored fairing with dummy guns has been fitted on the nose.

The first production model of the new twin-boom aircraft was designated simply the P-38 by the Army, whilst Lockheed called it their model 222. Latter-day historians sometimes refer to this aircraft as the P-38-LO, to prevent confusion with the generic P-38-type (LO standing for Lockheed's Burbank plant). So encouraging was the performance of the initial aircraft that construction of the P-38 began while the YP-38 was still under testing. While it is often stated that 30 P-38s were built, in fact 29 examples were produced, the first one being delivered in June 1941 and the last one two months later. The 19th P-38 on order, serial number 40-762, was instead completed as the one-off P-38A, which featured a pressurized cockpit.

The 29 P-38s bore Army Air Force serial numbers 40-744 through 40-761 and 40-763 through 40-773. These numbers corresponded to Lockheed construction numbers 222-2215 through 222-2232 and 222-2234 through 222-2244. Although it was not usually installed, the projected armament for the P-38 consisted of four .50-caliber machine guns and a 37mm cannon. Armor protection and bullet-resistant glass were provided for the pilot.

The type was clearly evolving into a more combat-worthy aircraft, especially given the protection for the pilot, but there would have to be many more changes before the P-38 was truly ready for battle.

It is also worth mentioning that at this point, the P-38 was known as the Atalanta, after the athletic and fierce Greek goddess – this in keeping with Lockheed's tradition of naming aircraft after mythological and celestial figures. When the British ordered the aircraft (the subsequent model 322), they assigned it the name "Lightning" – the name which was later universally adopted.

Coming in for a landing, the pilot of an unarmed P-38 has lowered the Fowler flaps and landing gear. As was the case on all models of the Lightning, there were flap sections inboard and outboard of the booms. The aircraft number 18 is painted in white on the nose.

A P-38-LO sits on a tarmac in front of a Western Air Express hangar. This example lacks serial-number markings. The upper mass balance on the horizontal stabilizer is visible. The P-38-LO was the first model of the Lightning to receive the Dark Olive Drab and Neutral Gray paint scheme at the factory. (National Museum of the United States Air Force.)

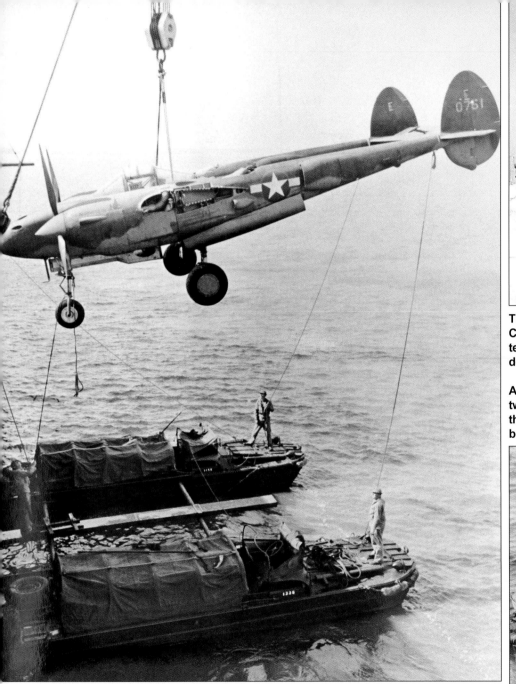

The DUKW dry-ferry rig delivers a de-winged P-38 to a beach off Charleston, South Carolina, during demonstrations in October 1943. To the far right, a man is exerting tension on the plane using a block and tackle, while men at the front of the plane pull it down the ramp.

A P-38, serial number 40-751, is ferried to a transport ship on a platform attached to two DUKWs. This aircraft lacks its guns as well as the large air scoops usually seen to the front of the turbo-superchargers on P-38s. It bears the national insignia with a red border authorized in late June 1943.

Wright Field in September 1943 asked GMC to develop an aircraft ferry apparatus for use with the DUKW. P-38, serial number 40-751, was used in these trials, and was ferried from a transport ship on a platform attached to two DUKWs. The outer wing sections have been removed from this P-38.

In 1940 the British and French ordered a significant quantity of P-38s, designated the Model 322-B for the British and Model 322-F for the French. The turbo-superchargers were to have been deleted from these models for the sake of simplicity, and they did not have counter-rotating propellers. After the defeat of France a few months later, the British assumed the entire contract, but, following contractual disputes with Lockheed concerning the quality of the aircraft, the British cancelled all but 143 of the Lightning Is, as they had redesignated the model. When the United States entered World War II, the U.S. Army Air Forces (USAAF) took over all of the Lightning I aircraft that had been cancelled by the British. Twenty-two of these, designated the P-322-I, retained the non-counter-rotating propellers and were used for testing and training, and 121 others, designated the P-322-II or RP-322-II (the R prefix, standing for "Restricted to noncombat use"), were converted to counter-rotating propellers by installing Allison V-1710-27 and -27m, F-2, engines and used for advanced trainers. At Chico Army Air Field, a training base for fighter pilots and bomber crews in California, an RP-322-I warms up its engines, with chocks still in place around its main landing gear wheels. The USAAF serial number, AF 207, is repeated in white on the nose and cowls, and in black under the left wing. The right propeller spinner is yellow and black, and the left hub is black and blue. (Stan Piet collection)

Due to contract disputes and the entry of the United States into World War II, the majority of the Lightning Mk I aircraft were taken over by the United States. Three of the aircraft, however, were sent to the British for evaluation purposes. The example shown here wears factory-applied British markings and camouflage. (Stan Piet collection)

This P-322-II was fitted with counter-rotating propellers, as is evident in the respective pitch angles of the propellers. The 138 P-322-IIs retained by the USAAF received new Allison V-1710F-2 engines at the Dallas Modification center. The USAAF serial number, AF 132, is painted in white on the nose. (National Archives)

This RP-322-II in U.S. markings and RAF camouflage and bearing serial number AF 103 was photographed at Shreveport, Louisiana, in January 1943. The projected armament for this model, two .50-caliber and two .30-caliber machine guns, was omitted. The nose gear was shorter than that of the YP-38, and the drag strut was relocated to the rear instead of the front of the main strut. (Stan Piet collection)

The P-38D (or P-38D-LO) program was an attempt to upgrade the Lightning to combat-capable status, although in fact the model failed to achieve that goal. The large white cross on the central nacelle of this P-38D marks it as part of Blue Force in the Carolina Maneuvers of 1941. The aircraft is securely tied to stakes in the ground to prevent its being flipped by high winds. Dummy guns are installed on the nose. Lockheed's model number for the P-38-D was the 222-62-08.

Although the additions of self-sealing fuel tanks and a low-pressure oxygen system were intended to render the next generation of P-38 – the P-38D – combat-ready, ultimately the Army did not deem it fit for such use. Instead, the aircraft was ultimately classified RP-38D, R being the designation for "Restricted to non-combat use." The 36 units produced were converted from the last of the P-38 production run and were delivered from August to October 1941. They carried USAAF serial numbers 40-774 to 40-809.

Armament, if installed, was normally four .50-caliber machine guns with nonstaggered barrels. A 37mm cannon was also projected but not installed. At the time, 37mm aircraft cannon were in extremely short supply, and this was the chief reason that the Lightnings were armed with the 20mm Hispano-Suiza cannon, beginning with the P-38E.

During the production of the P-38D, fillets were installed around the joint between the leading edge of the wing and the central nacelle joint to alleviate tail buffeting. The fairings for the wing/central nacelle joint, first introduced with the British Lightning I, were fitted to later P-38Ds. Although the P-38D was developed as a combat capable fighter, it was not to see much frontline service. Rather, it was used as a test bed for further improvements to the P-38 line and as a training and familiarization aircraft to enable pilots and ground crews to get accustomed to this revolutionary aircraft.

Much of this experience was gained by members of the 1st Pursuit Group, which received several of the P-38D models to augment the P-38s already in their hands, both of which types of aircraft were utilized in the fall 1941 Louisiana Maneuvers.

The number-one P-38D, serial 40-744 (tail number 0744), was modified with the removal of the turbo-superchargers and addition of a cockpit with canopy to the left boom. This was part of an experiment to gauge the medical and physical effects on a pilot positioned away from the centerline of a high-performance aircraft. There were no flight controls in the boom cockpit, as its purpose was only to house the human test subject.

Several Blue Force P-38s are seen at Randolph Field, Texas, wearing their markings for the 1941 Carolina Maneuvers. Individual aircraft numbers and "1P" for 1st Pursuit Group have been painted on the outsides of the vertical tails, and white crosses signifying Blue Force are painted on both wings and the front of the central nacelle.

This P-38D from the 1st Pursuit Group takes part in the Carolina Maneuvers in November 1941. The red cross marks it as part of the Red Force, the "enemy" component of the exercises, and the name *Snuffy* is painted on the nose. The "guns" are dummies. (Air Force Historical Research Agency)

The large air scoops on the booms in front of the turbo-superchargers were eliminated on the P-38E, and smaller supercharger cooling air intakes were installed instead. This P-38E, painted Dark Olive Drab on the upper surfaces and Neutral Gray on the undersides, has the aircraft number 14 painted in black on the outsides of the cowlings and a red band around each cowling to the rear of the propeller. The pitot tube is mounted on a mast to the front of the nose landing gear door. (Air Force Historical Research Agency)

Superficially, the P-38E strongly resembled its predecessor, the P-38D. But packed inside the familiar skin were more than 2,000 changes. The result of all this engineering was the first truly combat-ready Lightning. Four .50-caliber Colt-Browning MG 53-2 machine guns were also installed in the nose, but with staggered barrels. Improved instruments and hydraulic and electrical systems were added and a retractable landing light was mounted under the left wing. The drag strut of the nose landing gear was moved to the rear, allowing the main nose gear strut to be shortened: an innovation first applied to the Lightning I / P-322 series. This redesigned nose landing gear required less space in the nose of the P-38E than in the D. This additional space requirement allowed the gun bay to be redesigned, and the P-38 could carry almost double the ammunition borne by the P-38D. The P-38E was still powered by Allison V-1710-27 and -29, F-2, turbo supercharged engines rated at 1,150 horsepower each.

Lockheed's Burbank plant turned out a total of 210 P-38Es, which were delivered to the U.S. Army Air Forces between October 1941 and February 1942. Lockheed assigned the type its model number 222-62-09. Some examples saw combat in the Aleutian Islands, where Lightnings made their first kills of enemy aircraft on 4 August 1942. That day, Lt. Kenneth Ambrose and Lt. Stanley Long, flying two P-38Es of the 54th Fighter Squadron, shot down two Japanese H6K "Mavis" flying boats. Despite these successes, operation of the P-38 in the Aleutians highlighted shortcomings in the Lightning's cockpit heating system. At that time, fighters were typically heated by the engine, which in most designs was just ahead of the cockpit. Heating the Lightning's cockpit posed a challenge, however, since the pilot's position was comparatively remote from the aircraft's twin engines.

The P-38E airframe design also served as the basis for 99 F-4-1 reconnaissance aircraft, which were given Lockheed model number 222-62-13. Although many later reconnaissance planes were conversions from fighter aircraft, the F-4s were purpose-built on the assembly line for their role as eyes in the sky.

The first model of the Lightning to be produced in large quantity was the P-38E, also referred to as the P-38E-LO. The P-38E could achieve a speed of 395 miles per hour at 20,000 feet and was able to climb to an altitude of 20,000 feet in eight minutes. Behind the pilot was mounted an SCR-274N radio. (Air Force Historical Research Agency)

A key feature of the P-38E cockpit, and indeed of all Lightning cockpits, was the spoked control yoke on a control column mounted on the floor to the front right of the seat. Among the controls on the left side of the cockpit are those for the throttle, propeller, and fuel mixture, as well as the elevator tab control wheel. On the right side are circuit breakers and radio controls. At the top is the bulletproof glass panel.

The shiny oval object on the cowl to the front of the left wing of this P-38E is a highly polished metal surface that acted as a mirror so the pilot in the cockpit could visually ascertain if the landing gear was lowered. There was a similarly located "mirror" on the other cowling as well. On the underside of the front of the engine nacelles are two air inlets for the oil coolers. (Air Force Historical Research Agency)

Two crewmen watch as another man on the inboard wing section refuels a P-38E of the 54th Fighter Squadron in the Aleutians. To the left is the tanker truck with a fuel hose coming out of the rear compartment. (Stan Piet collection)

Pilots file out to a flight line of P-38s on Adak, in the Aleutians, in late 1944. The 54th Fighter Squadron was the only unit in the 343rd Fighter Group to fly Lightnings. It flew its first offensive missions against the Japanese in August 1942. (National Archives)

Following the Japanese invasion of Attu and Kiska Islands in the Aleutians in June 1942, the 54th Fighter Squadron joined several other fighter units of the 343rd Fighter Group, Eleventh Air Force, in combating the incursion. This P-38E, serial number 41-2239, was part of the 54th Fighter Squadron and was photographed at Longview Airfield on Adak toward the end of 1942. It is up on jacks for maintenance, with a jumble of tarps, toolboxes, and maintenance equipment around it.

In experiments to ascertain the practicality of converting the Lightning to a floatplane, Lockheed modified P-38E serial 41-1986 with upswept boom tails, to keep them clear of the water upon takeoff. The redesigned booms had a significantly taller profile where they met the vertical tails than was the case with stock P-38Es. Some sources have incorrectly identified this P-38E as an experiment to solve the problem of tail flutter.

To study streamlining, Lockheed converted P38-E, serial number 41-2048, into a flying test bed, its central nacelle extended fore and aft, and a rear cockpit fitted for an engineer/observer. The design of the extended central nacelle and the laminar-flow wing sections are revealed in this overhead view. A spray boom is attached to the rear of the left airfoil section.

This one-off plane, dubbed *Swordfish* or *Nosey,* first flew on 2 June 1943. Big airfoil sections were later added outboard of the twin booms to study laminar-flow airfoils and boundary-layer control. The engineer in the rear seat monitored the aerodynamic properties of the test airfoil on the left wing using sensors and instrumentation.

The F-4-1 was the first photo-reconnaissance version of the Lightning. Based on the P-38E, 99 F-4-1s were built. The guns were removed and two K-17 vertical cameras were installed in the nose. This is one of three examples that were supplied to the Royal Australian Air Force.

The cockpit layout of the F-4-1 resembled that of the P-38E, with some revisions, such as the intervalometer box to the immediate front of the seat. The intervalometer controlled the intervals between the openings of the shutter of the reconnaissance cameras.

F-4-1LO (P-38E airframe)

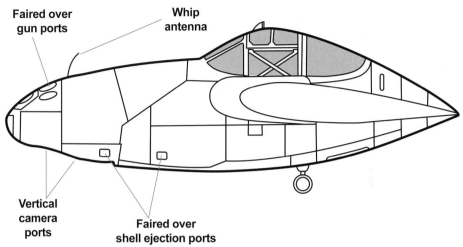

Faired over gun ports

Whip antenna

Vertical camera ports

Faired over shell ejection ports

The camera windows are visible under the nose of this F-4-1. Pylon-mounted drop tanks were added for extended range. The leading edges of the inboard wing sections have been removed, as have some of the cowling panels, exposing the engine control lines.

Several modifications differentiate the P-38F from the P-38E. The pitot tube and its mast were moved from under the nose to below the left wing on the P-38F, while the SCR-522-A antenna mast was mounted below the nose on the P-38F. (Stan Piet collection)

The P-38F featured numerous minor improvements over its predecessor, the P-38E. A fixed tab was incorporated into each aileron, and the engines were changed to the Allison V-1710-49 and -53, F-5, each with 1,325 horsepower. Three identification lights (front to back: red, blue-green, and amber) were installed toward the lower rear of the central nacelle. The P-38F was the first Lightning to be produced in multiple production blocks. These were the P-38F-LO (126 delivered), P-38F-1-LO (151), P-38F-5-LO (100), P-38F-13-LO (29), and P-38F-15-LO (121), for a total of 527. The P-38F-13-LO and -15-LO were originally British Lightning IIs that the USAAF took over.

Significantly, the center wing section of the P-38F was strengthened and two pylons were installed that permitted the carrying of bombs up to 1,000 pounds each, or perhaps more importantly, two external fuel tanks. These tanks came in two sizes, 75 and 165 gallons. The 165-gallon tank was designed by Kelly Johnson and was later adapted for use with numerous other aircraft. The doubling of fuel capacity greatly increased the aircraft's range, but the large tanks also presented operational challenges. Some maneuvers were prohibited with the tanks in place, and deciding when to release the tanks was also somewhat problematic. The tanks did not have fuel gauges, so it was difficult to determine exactly when they were nearing empty. Empty tanks could not be safely dropped at speeds over 160 m.p.h., although full tanks could be jettisoned at speeds up to 400 m.p.h.

Twenty F-4A-1 reconnaissance aircraft were produced concurrently with the P-38F.

Beyond the airframe changes, these reconnaissance aircraft differed from the previous F-4-1 in that cameras could be mounted obliquely as well as vertically in their noses.

Longshoremen steady the tail of a Lockheed P-38 as it is hoisted onto a trailer from a transport ship at New Caledonia on 27 September 1942. Drop tanks with two-color camouflage are mounted on the wing pylons. (National Archives)

Temporarily shorn of its outer wing sections, a U.S. Army Air Forces P-38 Lightning is transported by trailer on New Caledonia in the South Pacific. With the outer wing sections removed, it was easier to store more planes on transport ships. (National Archives)

A partially disassembled P-38 is transported on New Caledonia on 27 September 1942. The canopy, superchargers, and skin, wing, and control-surface joints are covered with protective materials, and the elevators and rudders are locked. (National Archives)

Assembly has just begun on these P-38Fs at the Lockheed plant. These were the center sections with the inboard wing sections. The unit at the lower left has not yet received the sections of the booms visible on the other units.

Sgt. Charles W. Craig and Pfc. Robert W. Hart, members of the 48th Service Squadron, straighten out a cowling panel of a 9th Fighter Squadron P-38 damaged in a forced landing at Strip No. 4, Dobodura, New Guinea, on 26 February 1943. (National Archives)

Two members of the 48th Service Squadron are repairing the port vertical tail of the same P-38 damaged while landing at Dobodura, New Guinea, on 26 February 1943. The boom is resting on an oil drum with several pieces of timber on top, with several sandbags on top of the boom to hold it down. The sergeant kneeling on the ground has detached the lower extension of the vertical fin. (National Archives)

Capt. Robert L. Faurot of the 39th Fighter Squadron, 35th Fighter Group, Fifth Air Force, poses next to his P-38F-5-LO, serial number 42-12623, at Port Moresby, New Guinea, on 20 January 1943. Capt. Faurot was killed in action on 3 March 1943. (National Archives)

The P-38F of the commander of the 50th Fighter Squadron warms up its engines at Camp Tripoli, near Reykjavík, Iceland, in preparation for taxi and take off on 16 March 1943.

On 6 July 1942, P-38s of the 27th Fighter Squadron, 1st Fighter Group, landed in Iceland. There they remained until they took off for Britain on 28 August. The visible tail numbers indicate that these were P-38F-1-LOs. The drop tanks needed for long flights are visible under several of the wings.

Marjorie Ann is a tired P-38F-5-LO, serial number 41-12570, relegated to squadron hack duties with the XV Fighter Command by June 1944, its guns and armor removed and its gun ports faired over. A squadron hack was usually a war-weary aircraft that was diverted to mundane chores, such as running errands between airfields. Painted white overall, the aircraft's red propeller spinners and nose show it to be with the Fifteenth Air Force in the Mediterranean Theater of Operations. Red is also applied to the wing tips and vertical tail. (Stan Piet collection)

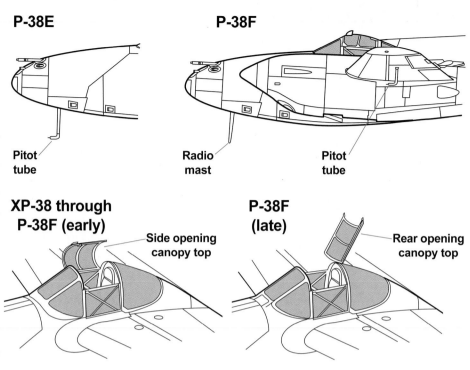

P-38 Lightning Specifications

	XP-38	YP-38	P-38	P-38D	P-38E	P-38F	P-38G	P-38H	P-38J	P-38L
Armament:	none fitted	none fitted	4 x .50 cal. MG + 1 x 37mm	4 x .50 cal MG	4 x .50 cal. MG + 1 x 20mm	4 x .50 cal. MG + 1 x 20mm	4 x .50 cal. MG + 1 x 20mm	4 x .50 cal. MG + 1 x 20mm	4 x .50 cal. MG + 1 x 20mm	4 x .50 cal. MG + 1 x 20mm
Bomb load:	none	none	none	none	none	2,000 lbs	3,200 lbs	3,200 lbs	4,000 lbs	4,000 lbs
Engines (2):	Allison V-1710-11/15, C-9	Allison V-1710-27/29, F-2	Allison V-1710-27/29, F-2	Allison V-1710-27/29, F-2	Allison V-1710-27/29, F-2	Allison V-1710-49/53, F-5	Allison V-1710-51/55, F-10	Allison V-1710-89/91, F-17	Allison V-1710-89/91	Allison V-1710-111/113
Max speed:	413 mph @ 20,000 ft	405 mph @ 20,000 ft	395 mph @ 20,000 ft	390 mph @ 20,000 ft	395 mph @ 20,000 ft	395 mph @ 25,000 ft	400 mph @ 25,000 ft	402 mph @ 25,000 ft	414 mph @ 25,000 ft	414 mph @ 25,000 ft
Cruise speed:		330 mph	310 mph	300 mph	300 mph	305 mph	340 mph	250 mph	290 mph	290 mph
Service ceiling:	38,000 feet	38,000 feet	38,000 feet	39,000 ft	39,000 ft	39,000 ft	39,000 ft	40,000 feet	44,000 feet	44,000 feet
Range:	1,390 miles	1,150 miles	1,490 miles	970 miles	975 miles	1,925 miles	2,400 miles	2,400 miles	2,600 miles	2,600 miles
Wing span:	52 ft	52 ft	52 ft	52 ft	52 ft	52 ft	52 ft	52 ft	52 ft	52 ft
Length:	37 ft 10 in	37 ft 10 in	37 ft 10 in	37 ft 10 in	37 ft 10 in	37 ft 10 in	37 ft 10 in	37 ft 10 in	37 ft 10 in	37 ft 10 in
Height:	12 ft 10 in	12 ft 10 in	12 ft 10 in	12 ft 10 in	12 ft 10 in	12 ft 10 in	12 ft 10 in	12 ft 10 in	12 ft 10 in	12 ft 10 in
Gross weight:	13,964 lbs	13,500 lbs	14,178 lbs	14,456 lbs	14,424 lbs	15,900 lbs	15,800 lbs	16,300 lbs	17,500 lbs	17,500 lbs
Number built/converted:	1	13	29	36	210 + 99 F-4-1	527 + 20 F-4A-1	1,082 + 180 F-5A	601	2,970 + 200 F-5B	3,810 + 113 built by Consolidated

The P-38G was the first model of the Lightning that the U.S. Army Air Forces acquired in numbers over one thousand. Outwardly it resembled the P-38F, with the main difference being new engine models: the Allison V-1710-51 and -55, F-10. Ground crewmen work on the wing of a P-38G as an officer, likely the pilot, stands in the cockpit. The aircraft number 1148 is visible on the side of the nose, underneath which is the radio mast. The rectangular shapes on the nacelle above the nose landing gear are the cartridge ejector chutes for the two right machine guns. (National Archives)

Like the P-38F, the P-38G was produced in several blocks: the P-38G-1-LO (80 delivered), P-38G-3-LO (12), P-38G-5-LO (68), P-38G-10-LO (548), P-38G-13-LO (174), and P-38G-15-LO (200), for a total of 1,082. The aircraft in blocks P-38G-1 through P-38G-10 were assigned the Lockheed model numbers 222-68-12, while those in blocks P-38G-13 and P-38G-15 were assigned model numbers 322-60-19. The difference is due to the latter having originally been ordered by the British as Lightning IIs. Starting with the P-38G-10-LO, the inboard wing sections were reinforced even further in order to bear the weight of a 2,000-pound bomb or 300-gallon drop tank (for long-range ferrying) under each wing.

Although these oversized tanks obviously brought about a significant increase in range, they were not used in combat, in part because they could not be jettisoned in flight without damage to the aircraft. In fact pilots were instructed to drop these tanks only in an emergency. With the addition of the capability of carrying first a pair of 165-gallon, then a pair of 300-gallon external tanks, the Lightning's low-pressure oxygen system had to be upgraded so that the pilot had the same endurance as his aircraft.

Yet again, a photo-recon version of this Lightning variant was produced. Designated F-5A, these 180 aircraft were produced on the assembly line alongside their armed sisters and were divided into three groups – 20 F-5A1, 20 F-5A-3 and 140 F-5A-10. The F-5A was given the Lockheed model number 222-68-16. While functionally equivalent to the earlier F-4A-1, the internal arrangement of the cameras was very different.

The P-38G model was the first version of which more than 1,000 units were produced. All P-38G models (as well as a few of the earlier models) were built on contract number 21217, which was issued in October 1941, and totaled $108,914,000.00.

A partially disassembled P-38G with weatherproofing materials applied is secured to the deck of an overseas-bound freighter. (Grumman Memorial Park via Leo Polaski)

Personnel assemble several Lightnings at a base in the South Pacific. The tail number of the nearest aircraft, 213501, marks it as a late P-38G-10-LO. This Lightning is raised on jack stands and the booms are supported by 55-gallon cans. (National Archives)

A British lorry tows a P-38G or P-38H from the Liverpool docks to Speke Airfield. The Lightning's wings will be reinstalled at the Lockheed British Reassembly Division plant at Speke. The props have been removed and the cowlings covered.

Along with the upgraded power plants, the P-38G featured improved engine controls that optimized the long-range, high-speed cruising characteristics of the aircraft. Also included was an improved low-pressure oxygen system with greater capacity.

A Federal Aircraft ski kit is fitted to the landing struts of this P-38G for testing takeoffs and landings in Arctic conditions at Ladd Field, Alaska, in early 1944. The skis were retractable, and the landing bay doors were removed. The tests showed that landing and takeoff with the skis were feasible, but the project was not pursued. The pilot's retractable step dangles below the central nacelle.

Mackie was the P-38G-10-LO, USAAF serial number 42-12926, of Capt. Harry J. Dayhuff, 82nd Fighter Squadron. Mackie was the nickname of his wife. The name *Mike* was also painted on the right cowling. The two white bands on the boom signify it was the squadron commander's aircraft. The national insignia has a yellow border, perhaps applied when the 82nd Fighter Squadron's Lightnings were sent to North Africa in early 1943. The 82nd kept its P-38s until February 1943, when the unit was reequipped with P-47s.

A P-38G numbered 83 is armed with a 100-pound bomb on the pylon.

An F-5A photo-reconnaissance Lightning undergoes maintenance in Tunis, Tunisia, in August 1943. Based on the P-38G airframe, the F-5A featured on the left side of the nose a quadrilateral window and a smaller rectangular window (aft of the tiger's mouth) for oblique cameras, as well as windows on the underside of the nose for vertical cameras. A name, evidently *Skyhawk,* is painted above the quadrilateral window. The pitot tube has been relocated to below the left wing, and the antenna mast is on top of the nose. (Stan Piet collection)

An F-5A photo-reconnaissance Lightning prepares to take off on a mission from a dirt runway in North Africa. Instead of a quadrilateral window on the right door of the camera compartment, a smaller, rectangular window is below the door. The aircraft is painted in the Synthetic Haze paint developed for photo-reconnaissance Lightnings in 1943. This camouflage scheme entailed spraying a base coat of synthetic Sky Base Blue overall, with synthetic Flight Blue sprayed in shadowed areas and on the sides, giving the aircraft a subtly mottled effect. (National Archives)

Two ground crewmen stand proudly in front of an F-5A of the 90th Photographic Reconnaissance Wing parked in a revetment in North Africa. In addition to the quadrilateral and rectangular windows for oblique cameras, three windows of different sizes for vertical cameras are on the bottom of the nose. Production of the F-5As was in three blocks: the F-5A-1-LO (20 built) based on the P-38G-1-LO airframe, F-5A-3-LO (20 built) based on the P-38G-3-LO airframe, and F-5A-10-LO (140 built) based on the P-38G-10-LO airframe. (National Archives)

GR 2/33 of the Free French Air Force operated this F-5A from al-Marsá ("La Marsa"), Tunisia, in 1943.

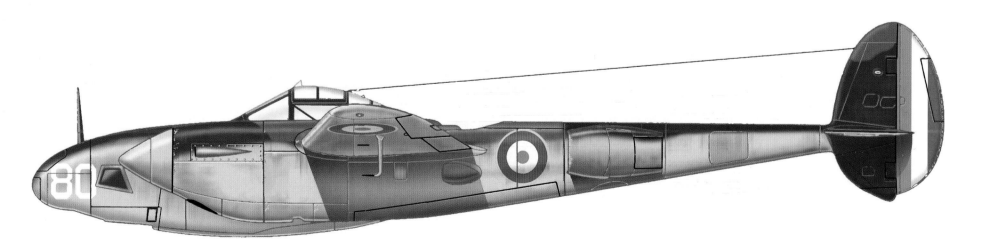

Lightnings of the 90th Photographic Reconnaissance Wing undergo maintenance at an airfield in North Africa in 1943. Although the original USAAF caption identified the aircraft as F-4s, the plane in the background has the quadrilateral window and lower oblique window characteristic of the F-5A. Both aircraft are painted in the Synthetic Haze scheme. (National Archives)

The pilot of *Stinky 2,* an F-5A-10-LO, enters the cockpit while a t-shirted ground crewman stands by. This photo-reconnaissance Lightning was with the 9th Photographic Reconnaissance Squadron, 9th Bomb Group, in India toward the end of 1943. Several numbers are painted on this oil-streaked, weather-beaten aircraft, including 7735 above the black 301 on the nose, and P14A over 40 on the tail. (National Archives)

F-5A-10s often carried names or nose art. The national insignia on the aircraft nicknamed *Stinky 2* had the red surround used for a short time in 1943. The aircraft was assigned to the 9th Photographic Reconnaissance Squadron, which was attached to the 7th Bomb Group and based in Pandaveswar, India, in 1943.

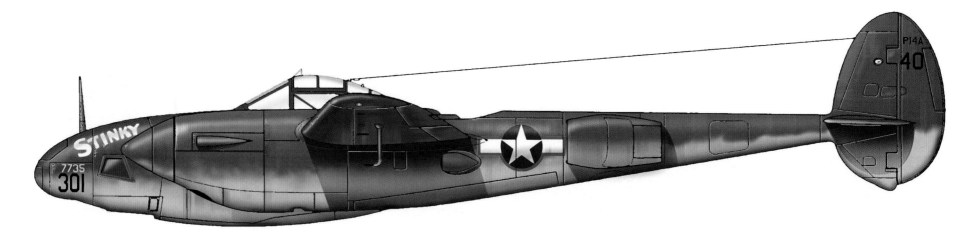

The P-38H was similar to the P-38G, with the main difference being that the H model had the more powerful Allison V-1710-89 and -91, F-17, engines. Each engine was rated at 1,425 horsepower, but in actual use they were limited to 1,240 horsepower because the cooling system was insufficient to cope with engine heat at the maximum-rated power. Even with this, single-engine operation of the P-38 was possible, although single-engine turns were of sufficient concern to prompt Lockheed to send their company pilots into the field to provide demonstrations, even devoting issue No. 3 of the company publication *Hangar Flying* to the subject. In this photo, the P-38H-5-LO cruises with the left engine off and the propeller feathered. (Stan Piet collection)

Manufactured in the summer of 1943, this late-production P-38H-5-LO undergoes a test run. It wears the national insignia with red border that was briefly authorized in the summer of that year. (Stan Piet collection)

In response to reports by P-38 combat pilots that they were experiencing reduced engine power above 25,000 feet, Lockheed engineers devised automatic shutters for the oil coolers and radiators of the P-38H. Automatic controls were added to the turbo-superchargers, and the problem of leakage in the intercoolers mounted in the leading edges of the outer wing sections, a long-standing difficulty, was reduced.

Underwing bomb and drop-tank capacity was upgraded to 3,200 pounds. Beginning with the P-38H-5-LO, the improved B-33 turbo-superchargers were installed. Despite these improvements, it would take the major reworking of the coolant system in the P-38J to finally allow the V-1710-89 and -91 engines to work at their full potential. The first P-38H-1-LO served as prototype for the new model, and it, along with ten P-38J-1-LO prototypes, was ordered on contract AC-21217. There were only two production blocks for the P-38H: the P-38H-1-LO, with 226 examples delivered, including the prototype; and P-38H-5-LO, with 375 delivered, for a total of 601. Unlike many previous models, no photo reconnaissance variants of the P-38H were included in the orders placed with Lockheed. Nor do any official records exist that suggest that such aircraft were created in the field.

The armament of the P-38H differed from that of the P-38E through G in that the 20mm M1 cannon was replaced by the 20mm M2C cannon. The two cannon differed primarily in method of manufacture, and the M2 receiver was 0.2 inches longer than that of the M1. The M1 receiver slide was riveted, whereas the M2 was bolted. Both guns had a cyclic rate of fire of 600-700 rounds per minute and a muzzle velocity of 2,850-2,950 feet per second.

The P-38H marked the end of the Lightnings that featured the smoothly contoured engine-nacelle chins with two flush, rounded air inlets for the oil coolers. On the wing pylons are two 1,000-pound general-purpose bombs. (Dyersburg Army Air Base Memorial Association)

The same P-38H-5-LO shown on the previous page is viewed here from a different angle. In addition to a redesigned engine nacelle chin, the next model in the Lightning series, the P-38J, would have redesigned radiator housings on the booms. (Stan Piet collection)

A Lockheed test pilot shows off the ability of a P-38H-5-LO to fly on one engine. Exhaust stains emanate from the louvered vents to the front of the turbo-superchargers and from the exhaust gates on the rears of the superchargers. The one visible drop tank was painted Dark Olive Drab on top and Neutral Gray on the bottom. (Stan Piet collection)

Number 923 is painted Dark Olive Drab and Neutral Gray, with yellow spinners. Faintly painted on the nose is the number 1434. The tail number, 266923, indicates this is a P38H-5-LO. Under the engine nacelle, the outlet vent for the oil coolers is lowered. (Dyersburg Army Air Base Memorial Association)

Retractable lights under both wings were introduced on the P-38F, and dual lights appear on this P-38H. The polished metal mirror that enabled the pilot to see if the landing gear was lowered is visible on the inboard side of the right cowling. (Dyersburg Army Air Base Memorial Association)

Of these three lines in the Lockheed factory, the line to the right is where the Lightnings undergo initial assembly. On the center line, wings and engines are installed. The left line was where final components were assembled. Following completion in this building, the P-38s were shuttled to the paint hangar to receive their camouflage.

Crewmen maintain *Pluto,* a P-38H-1-LO, number 42-66683, of the 12th Fighter Squadron in the Southwest Pacific. The Japanese flag denotes an aircraft kill. (National Archives)

On the Lockheed assembly line, Allison quick-exchange engine units (QECs) are massed, ready to be installed on the P-38 airframes to the left. The QECs included the engine-bearing frames and struts, which would be attached to the structural frames of the engine nacelles. Lockheed opened a new assembly plant during P-38 production. The company claimed that the new plant had a daily output double that of the preceding facility.

39

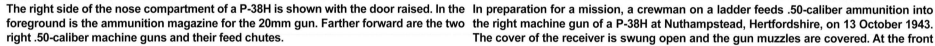

The right side of the nose compartment of a P-38H is shown with the door raised. In the foreground is the ammunition magazine for the 20mm gun. Farther forward are the two right .50-caliber machine guns and their feed chutes.

1st Lt. H. A. Blood of the 14th Fighter Group inspects belted 20mm ammunition before it is loaded in the 150-round magazine in front of him. The weapons bay doors of *Babe,* a P-38H, are both open, and the .50-caliber machine gun barrels lack the protective covers often observed over them when the aircraft are on the ground. (National Archives)

In preparation for a mission, a crewman on a ladder feeds .50-caliber ammunition into the right machine gun of a P-38H at Nuthampstead, Hertfordshire, on 13 October 1943. The cover of the receiver is swung open and the gun muzzles are covered. At the front of the nose is the gun camera port. (National Archives)

This is a pilot's-eye view of a P-38H cockpit. At the top is the gun sight, to the front of a panel of bulletproof glass. To the left of center of the instrument panel is the charging handle for the nose guns. In the right foreground are the control column and yoke.

Lightning number 164 of the 475th Fighter Group, most likely a P-38H, was assigned to Maj. George W. Prentice, first commander of that group. While he was in command of the 475th, the group was based in Australia and subsequently was transferred to New Guinea. Prentice had formerly commanded the first unit in the Southwest Pacific to fly P-38s, the 39th Fighter Squadron.

A P-38H that experienced a crash landing has been loaded onto a dolly for removal. A drop tank is still in place and the muzzles of the guns are covered.

Capt. Jerry H. Ayers, second from right, poses with his ground crew by his P-38H, *Mountain Ayers,* of the 38th Fighter Squadron at Nuthampstead, England, in 1943. The nose art was by Sgt. Robert Sand, who recalled painting on the squadron's planes on cold nights after his regular work was finished. (Stan Piet collection)

Ground crew inspect a P-38H of the 55th Fighter Group after it landed at Wormingford in Essex, England. It had collided with another fighter in its squadron during a dogfight with the enemy; the other P-38 did not survive. (Sgt. Robert Sand / Stan Piet collection)

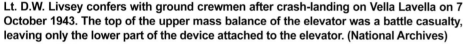

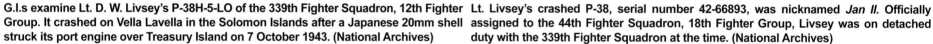

G.I.s examine Lt. D. W. Livsey's P-38H-5-LO of the 339th Fighter Squadron, 12th Fighter Group. It crashed on Vella Lavella in the Solomon Islands after a Japanese 20mm shell struck its port engine over Treasury Island on 7 October 1943. (National Archives)

Lt. D.W. Livsey confers with ground crewmen after crash-landing on Vella Lavella on 7 October 1943. The top of the upper mass balance of the elevator was a battle casualty, leaving only the lower part of the device attached to the elevator. (National Archives)

Lt. Livsey's crashed P-38, serial number 42-66893, was nicknamed *Jan II*. Officially assigned to the 44th Fighter Squadron, 18th Fighter Group, Livsey was on detached duty with the 339th Fighter Squadron at the time. (National Archives)

To better adapt P-38s as formation bombers, the Army Air Forces developed the idea of fitting certain P-38s with clear bombardier's noses and Norden bombsights. To develop the design, a wooden nose simulating the final shape was grafted onto this P-38H-5-LO.

The P-38J represented a new look for the Lightning, with its deep-chinned engine nacelles and, starting with the P-38J-10-LO, a redesigned windshield with a flat, bulletproof glass panel in the center. This example, a P-38J-10-LO, was photographed during a check flight over Southern California, and is wearing no markings other than its serial number and national insignia.

The P-38J incorporated numerous changes that gave it a distinctly different look from its predecessors. In order to allow the Allison V-1710-89 and -91 engines to meet their full performance potential, the intercooling system was revamped. Intercooling is used on many supercharged engines to lower the intake air temperature in order to prevent pre-detonation (knocking), which is very destructive to engine components. The intercoolers that had previously been mounted inside the leading edges of the outer wings were eliminated in favor of core-type intercoolers housed in a redesigned engine-nacelle chin. On either side of the intercooler intake on each chin was an intake for the oil coolers.

To take advantage of the vacated space behind the leading edges of the outer wings, partway through the production of the P-38J a fuel tank was installed inside the leading edge of each outer wing, with a filler cap located on top of each wing. The ailerons received a hydraulic boost system, and the movable trim tabs were discontinued. Cockpit heating and defrosting equipment was improved, fuses were replaced with circuit breakers, and the round control yoke in the cockpit gave way to a new yoke with two pistol-type grips. Starting with the P-38J-10-LO, the curved windshield was eliminated in favor of one with a flat bulletproof glass front panel. Six blocks of this model were produced from the P-38J-1-LO to the P-38J-25-LO, with a total of 2,970 built.

The P-38J-25-LO also finally resolved the compressibility problem that had been discovered with the YP-38. The difficulty was solved by adding a set of pilot-operated compressibility flaps just outboard of the engines.

The mount of many notable Lightning aces, including Dick Bong and Tom McGuire, the P-38J truly brought the Lightning into its own as a combat aircraft.

From what is visible of its tail number, this Lightning is a P-38J-10-LO. The number 23280, which is not associated with any part of the tail number, is stenciled on the side of the nose. The shapes of the new chin scoops appear to good advantage.

Boom Development

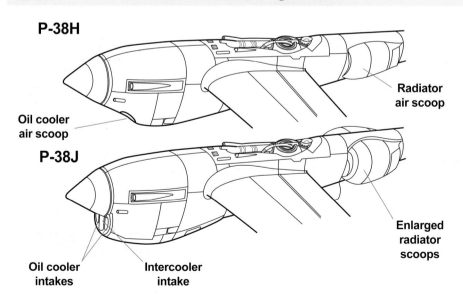

P-38H

P-38J

Oil cooler air scoop

Radiator air scoop

Enlarged radiator scoops

Oil cooler intakes

Intercooler intake

Canopy Development

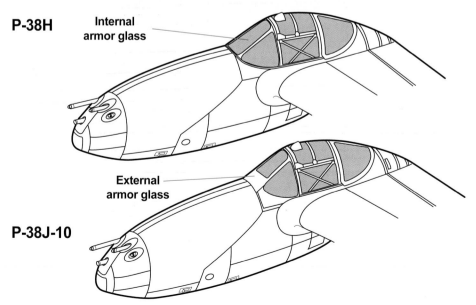

P-38H

P-38J-10

Internal armor glass

External armor glass

To commemorate the 5,000th P-38 to be completed at Lockheed's Burbank factory, the company gave this fully armed P-38J-20-LO a bright red paint job and named it *Yippee*. Milo Burcham, chief test pilot for Lockheed, warms up the engines of *Yippee* prior to takeoff. In addition to the plane's overall red paint job, which evidently had a slight orange cast, the aircraft exhibited light gray paint on the landing gear (except the bright, natural-metal oleo cylinder) and landing gear door. The seemingly ever-present polished metal mirror on the side of the engine nacelle is in view. As chief test pilot, Burcham played pivotal roles in the development of the P-38 and the training of Lockheed test pilots. He was killed taking off on a test flight of the new YP-80 at the Lockheed Air Terminal in Burbank, California, on 20 October 1944. (Stan Piet collection)

Test pilot Milo Burcham demonstrates flying *Yippee* with the left engine off and the propeller feathered. Burcham's single-engine flight routine relieved many pilots' concerns about the P-38's capabilities. Born in 1903, Burcham became a flight instructor in the 1930s. In 1933 he set an inverted flight endurance record of over four hours, and that record was not broken until the 1990s. Lockheed hired Burcham as a production test pilot in 1941, and he became the company's chief test pilot soon thereafter. In January 1944 he flew the first test flight of the army's prototype jet fighter, the XP-80 Shooting Star, and he was closely identified with the early testing of that pioneering aircraft. Among his many accomplishments during World War II was designing a training course to teach students how to fly the P-38 with one engine out at low speed and altitude.

Milo Burcham flies *Yippee* over Southern California on 17 May 1944. The name *Yippee* appeared on both sides of the nose as well as on the undersides of the wings. The frame of the canopy was left in bare-metal finish. (Stan Piet collection)

Milo Burcham, chief test pilot for Lockheed, poses on the wing of *Yippee* on the Lockheed ramp at Burbank, California, on 17 May 1944. Bomb pylons were installed on the Lightning. (Stan Piet collection)

A Lockheed test pilot takes one of the 790 P-38J-10-LOs on a flight over the Southern California hills. This sub-model of Lightning was produced from October to December 1943 and was the first sub-model to be fitted with flat bulletproof glass windshields. (Stan Piet collection)

Mechanics with "Lockheed Service" written on their coveralls make adjustments to the right engine of a P-38J-15-LO. Some parts of the internal framework of the engine nacelle, to which the cowling panels were fastened, are painted interior green, while other parts of it are bare metal. The discs on the wheels were often removed in operational service. (Stan Piet collection)

A test pilot takes the first P38J-15-LO through its paces. In the final months of World War II, it became increasingly the practice for Lockheed to deliver Lightnings to the U.S. Army Air Forces in bare-aluminum finishes instead of camouflage paint. (Stan Piet collection)

A P-38J-15-LO, tail number 328859, makes a test flight over water. The radiator housings on the P-38J were larger and of different contours than those on the preceding P-38 models. Although the mass balances on the elevator had been proven to be ineffective, they remained on the P-38J and subsequent models. (Stan Piet collection)

With the right cowling side panels removed, the outboard oil cooler is visible behind its intake on the chin. The center intake is for the intercooler. Near the top of the engine, above the diagonal engine bearer strut, is the exhaust manifold. The turbo-supercharger ram intake is below the wing.

Ninth Air Force mechanics repair a P-38 engine at a base in Belgium. With the cowling panels off, the engine and the structure nacelle are visible. Below the black valve cover is the exhaust manifold. (National Archives)

In a hangar of the 467th Service Squadron on 23 July 1944, the crane of an aircraft wrecker supports the left wing of a P-38J (via a beam with a protective strip of canvas over it) while an overhead hoist supports the central nacelle. (National Archives)

Following the crash landing of a P-38J, a Federal Model 606 7½-ton C2 aircraft wrecker is backed up to the Lightning and preparing to recover it with its boom.

A ground crewman positions a jack stand under the left wing of a P-38J-20-LO, serial 44-23974, while the jack stand under the right has been extended. Men sit on the horizontal stabilizer to balance the front-heavy P-38. To the front of the wing pylon is a gun camera fairing, a retrofit, since the P-38L was the first model with this feature. (National Archives)

When a B-17 rear-ended a fighter plane on a ramp, the result could only be catastrophic. Somehow, this Flying Fortress collided with a P-38J, the propellers chewing up the boom and wing and, no doubt, other parts of the Lightning.

In Belgium, crewmen repair *Mary Rose II*, a 485th Fighter Squadron P-38J-5-LO. A mobile maintenance shop in a 6x6 truck is backed up to a wooden platform, allowing men servicing the engine to access parts and equipment. (National Archives)

Four ground crewmen pose with *Journey's End*, P-38J-20-LO USAAF serial number 42-67685 and fuselage code CG-V, assigned to the 38th Fighter Squadron, 55th Fighter Group, Eighth Air Force. The plane was flown by Lt. Col. Joseph Myers Jr. (Stan Piet collection)

The nose landing gear was an Achilles' heel of P-38s, including this P-38J-5-LO, which has crashed upon landing.

51

Armorers hoist a general-purpose bomb to the port pylon of a P-38. Bomb hoists are installed on each side of the pylon, attached to which are a steel cable and a sling. When the bomb reached the desired height, it was shackled the pylon. (National Archives)

Mary Rose II was a P-38J-5-LO with the 370th Fighter Group, 485th Fighter Squadron, Ninth Air Force. *Winnie* is painted on the left cowling, and black and white invasion stripes are present. The 7F code and triangle on the tail were the squadron's markings.

Armorers wheel a bomb to *Irish Lassie,* a P-38J piloted by Lt. W. G. Baumeister of the "Twin-Tailed Dragons," 459th Fighter Squadron of the 80th Fighter Group. Based at Chittagong, India, (now in Bangladesh) the squadron racked up an impressive record against Japanese aircraft in Burma (now Myanmar).

Both the nose and left main landing gears collapsed when this P-38J tried to land in a boggy field.

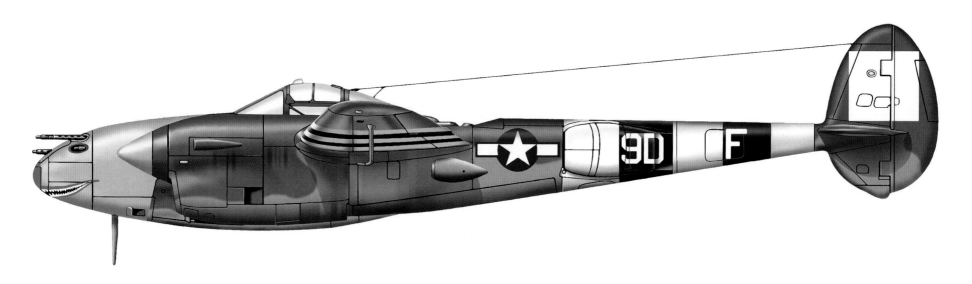

Black and white invasion stripes were painted all the way around the wings and booms for identification purposes in preparation for the invasion of Normandy on 6 June 1944. This P-38J was assigned to the 485th Fighter Squadron of the 370th Fighter Group, which was part of the 9th Air Force in England.

Crews at a South Pacific base reassemble Lightnings that have been shipped in partially disassembled, prior to sending them to the front. In the background is a Lightning with its outer wings yet to be installed. Several sets of uninstalled outer wings are visible to the right of the makeshift hoisting frames in the left background. (National Archives)

A P-38J is prepared for shipment overseas by Dade Packaging. Workers remove the bolts fastening the outer wing to the engine nacelle to make for a more compact storage width on the deck of a ship. The propeller is removed, as are several cowl panels to provide a better view of the engine. (Grumman Memorial Park via Leo Polaski)

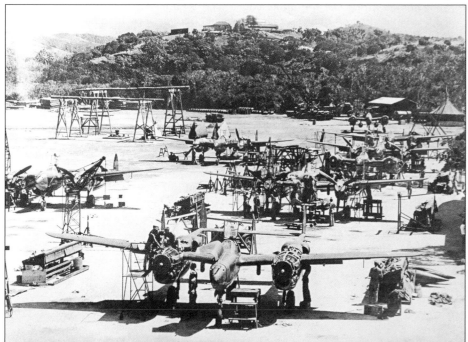

A P-38J-10-LO undergoing maintenance at a base in the Pacific is serving double duty as a drying rack for laundry. The sign on the left tent identifies it as the armaments shop of the 11th Airdrome Squadron, and the sign on the tent at the center indicates that it is the squadron radio shop.

P-38J serial number 43-28466, piloted by Albert J. Reid and based at Santa Maria Army Airfield, California, suffered a ground accident caused by mechanical failure on 4 September 1944. Apparently the nose landing gear collapsed, causing the nose to plow into the ground. The Lightning was repaired but suffered another accident on 28 January 1945, involving pilot Robert C. Black at Santa Rosa Army Airfield, California.

Seen here in Chittagong, India, (now Bangladesh) in 1944, the P-38J-10-LO of Major Willard J. Webb of the 459th Fighter Squadron, the "Twin-Tailed Dragons," was the first Lightning in the China-Burma-India Theater to be fitted with AC-MIC 4.5-inch rocket launchers for air-to-ground attack. The tubes were mounted in trios on each side of the central nacelle, and each rocket contained a 39-pound high-explosive warhead. On the cowling and boom is the squadron's distinctive dragon design. (National Archives)

A P-38J named *Pretty Gal* warms its engines on a ramp. Another new feature of the P-38J series was the oil cooler exhausts, visible here as a rectangular shape on the lower side of the cowling. (National Archives)

A P-38J assigned to the 9th Fighter Squadron, 82nd Bomb Group, Fifteenth Air Force in Italy has just released two bombs. Two more bombs are visible under the wings near the fuselage. The 9th Fighter Squadron was prominent in the Ploeşti raid of 10 June 1944. (National Archives via Stan Piet)

Armorer Cpl. Joe Diaz inspects an ammunition belt being fed into the magazine of the Hispano 20mm cannon of a late-model P-38, named *Li'l Venus.* Ammo belts for the .50-caliber machine guns hang from their trays, as the maintenance manuals termed them. The nose fairing for the 20mm gun barrel has been removed. (National Archives)

Having opened the receiver cover of the right .50-caliber machine gun, an armorer feeds ammunition into the receiver. He has pulled out the ammunition tray for that gun for loading purposes. The two T-shaped objects to the lower front of the 150-round 20mm ammunition magazine are the stowed machine gun charger handles. (National Archives)

At a base in Belgium late in 1944 or 1945, mechanics methodically disassemble a P-38. A host of details of the internal construction of a P-38 are visible, from the framing and structural members of the weapons bay at the left, to the engine bearings at the center. (National Archives)

56

This P-38J-10-LO of the Ninth Air Force received credit for being the first Lighting to land in France following the invasion. It sits on a landing strip adjacent to a beachhead, a canvas cover thrown over the top of the canopy. Above the tail number is a smaller number 29. A censor evidently scratched and inked out some of the landing craft in the center. (Air Force Historical Research Agency)

A Lt. Kunz poses by his P-38J-15-LO, *Napoleon's Delight 'NIN'* in Belgium on 24 December 1944. The artwork is painted on fabric that has been pasted on the weapons-bay door. To Kunz's rear is the aircraft's nomenclature and data stencil. (National Archives)

Jimmy II, a P-38J with the 485th Fighter Squadron, 370th Fighter Group, Ninth Air Force, is parked on a ramp next to bombed-out buildings during the group's advance across northwestern Europe in the final months of war. *"Pride"* is painted on the left cowling. The *"FS"* on the boom and black triangle on the tail are the squadron's markings.

The base of the Eiffel Tower provided a picturesque setting for reassembling a P-38 for display purposes following the Liberation of Paris. The right outer wing section is on the truck to the right. Judging from the visible last four digits of its tail number, it was probably a P-38J-25-LO. Next to the Lightning sits a P-47D-26-RA Thunderbolt.

57

Captain Herschel "Easy" Ezell, Jr., was the bombardier of this P-38J Droop Snoot 42-67450, *Eze Does it.* Ezell was assigned to the 77th Fighter Squadron, 20th Fighter Group, flying from Kings Cliffe, England.

Lockheed developed a bomber version of the Lightning, the P-38J Droop Snoot. This example was dubbed *Colorado Belle.* The guns were removed from the nose, and a Plexiglas bomber nose and a bombardier's position with a Norden bomb sight were installed. A Droop Snoot acted as a guide bomber, with other P-38s in the formation dropping their bombs on cue. Lockheed produced 23 Droop Snoots on its assembly line and delivered 100 Droop Snoot conversion kits to the USAAF.

A droop-snoot P-38 rests at an airfield in Belgium. The bombardier had entry/exit hatches at the top of his compartment and at the bottom of the compartment to the front of the nose landing gear. Inside the cramped compartment, the bombardier had a seat and Norden bombsight. For visibility, he had the clear nose with an optically flat clear panel on the lower front, plus a window on each side of the compartment. (National Archives)

This P-38J Droop Snoot bears the "F5" fuselage code of the 428th Fighter Squadron, 474th Fighter Group, serving with the Ninth Air Force in the European Theater, 1944-1945. The bombardier's compartment in the nose was very confined, but the clear nose provided a good, clear view of the battlespace in addition to having a flat optical panel through which the bombardier sighted the Norden bomb sight.

A P-38J Droop Snoot Lightning is parked at RAF Horsham St. Faith, near Norwich, Norfolk, England, in March 1945 in the final days of World War II in Europe. The clear panel at the top of the bombardier's compartment is visible through the clear nose. The plane bears a dull natural-metal finish.

Ground crewmen on a rest break on Tinian take advantage of the sparse shade offered by a P-38J with the 318th Fighter Group. This group had inherited its P-38s from the 21st Fighter Group in November 1944, and this Lightning was visiting Tinian from its home base at East Field on Saipan, just a few miles away. (Stan Piet collection)

A line of Lightnings at an airfield on Tinian includes in the foreground a late-production P-38J, the nickname of which appears to be *He 'Ul Dawg!* of the 318th Fighter Group. The nose art consists of a dog's head, painted light beige. The spinner on that P-38J is red, while those on the other aircraft are black. (Stan Piet collection)

The little-known *Down Beat* was a loaner Lockheed P-38J-15 Lightning flown by Maj. Dick Bong while he was with the Fifth Fighter Command based at Nadzab, New Guinea, in April 1944. While flying *Down Beat,* Bong downed three Nakajima Ki-43 "Oscars," making him the first to surpass Eddie Rickenbacker's U.S. record of 26 kills during World War I.

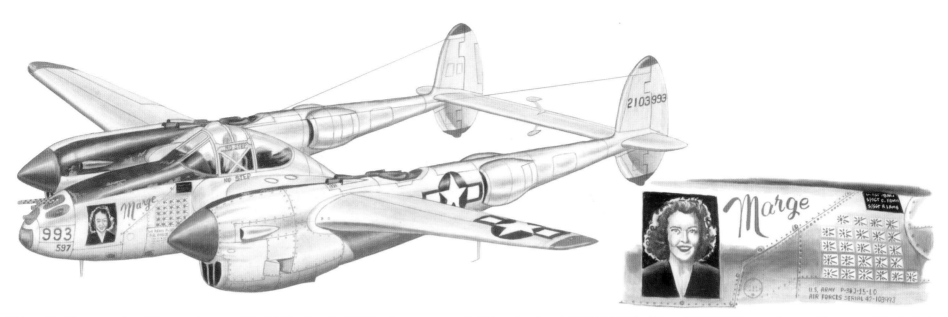

Richard Ira Bong was the U.S. ace of aces of World War II, with 40 kills of enemy aircraft. This natural-metal P-38J-15-LO, *Marge* (42-103993), was the most famous of Capt. Dick Bong's fighters. He flew this red-trimmed Lightning while with the Fifth Fighter Command stationed at Cape Gloucester in March of 1944. Access panels around the gun barrels were also red. A photograph of Marge Vattendahl, Bong's fiancée, was displayed beside the red kill marks on the aircraft's nose.

Bong's name is closely associated with the P-38, as he gained all of his victories in Lightnings. He racked up his kills in several different P-38s, including this P-38J-15-LO, USAAF serial number 42-104380, seen in Nadzab, New Guinea, in about April 1944. (Stan Piet collection)

The second-highest-scoring U.S. ace of World War II after Richard Bong was Maj. Thomas B. McGuire Jr., who commanded the 431st Fighter Squadron. Killed over Negros Island, the Philippines, on 7 January 1945, he flew a series of P-38s dubbed *Pudgy,* including *Pudgy III,* his mount from March 1944 to August 1944. (Stan Piet collection)

A P-38J served as the prototype of the Pathfinder, equipped not with a Norden bomb sight, but with the "Mickey" AN/APS-15 BTO (bombing through overcast) radar inside a large, blunt plastic radome in the nose. The radar operator sat between the radome and the cockpit, and he had a window on each side. Subsequent Pathfinders were converted from P-38L airframes. (San Diego Air and Space Museum)

Several different types of Lightning are lined up on the ramp at Lockheed's Burbank plant, receiving some final details before delivery. The second plane from the left is an F-5E in a Synthetic Haze camouflage scheme. Here again, the small window for the right oblique camera, below the camera bay door, appears to be wearing its protective contact film and is oversprayed with the Synthetic Haze. (Stan Piet collection)

Lockheed took advantage of the extended range and enhanced performance of the new P-38J airframe by using it as the basis for an improved series of photo-reconnaissance Lightnings: the F-5B-1-LO, F-5C-1-LO, F-5E-2-LO, and F-5E-3-LO. The F-5B-1-LO was built as such on the assembly line, while the other three sub-models were converted from P-38Js. The later, but very similar, F-5E-4 aircraft were converted from P-38L fighters.

The F-5B-1-LO was the first Lightning to incorporate the Sperry auto-pilot. Although mounted on a P-38J airframe, the camera nose of the F-5B-1-LO was similar in shape and in the arrangement of its camera windows to the camera nose of the F-5A. The nose contained three camera bays in which four different camera combinations could be installed. The cameras themselves were selected from the 6-inch K-17 chart camera, 12-inch or 24-inch K-17 vertical camera, and 24-inch K-18 vertical camera. In each of the typical installations, a K-17 6-inch oblique chart camera was mounted in the extreme forward position. In the center bay would be two 6-inch K-17 chart cameras or a single 12- or 24-inch K-17 chart camera. The rear-most bay would hold reconnaissance cameras, either a 24-inch K-18 or a pair of 24-inch K-17s.

In all, 200 F-5B-1-LOs were produced. They were assigned army serial numbers 42-67312 through 42-67401 and 42-68192 through 42-68301. Model 422-81-21 was Lockheed's designation for the F-5B-1-LO. Model designations 422-81-20, 422-81-22 and 422-81-23 were assigned to the F-5C-1-LO, F-5E-2-LO, and F-5E-3-LO aircraft respectively, all of which were converted from P-38J production fighters. A total of 100 P-38J-15-LO aircraft were converted to the F-5E-2. Among the users of the F-5B was the U.S. Navy, which operated four of them in North Africa. The Navy designated the type FO-1, and operated the aircraft exclusively from land bases, never from aircraft carriers. Lockheed did propose a carrier-based, folding-wing variant of the Lightning – their model 822 – but in part due to the Navy's preference for air-cooled engines, this project never advanced beyond the design stage.

During World War II, the haze paint for photo-reconnaissance Lightnings underwent several changes in its formulation and the manner in which it was applied, and there were noticeable variations in the appearance of the Synthetic Haze camouflage schemes. (Stan Piet collection)

This is one of 200 F-5B-1-LOs built in the first of two production blocks, in September-October 1943. The second production block of F-5B-1-LOs was produced in December 1943. The red-bordered national insignia was authorized briefly from June to August 1943. (Stan Piet collection)

The right side of the F-5B-1-LO seen on the previous page appears here on a test flight with a P-38J-5-LO in the background. One of the two small windows on the right side of the nose for oblique cameras is visible below the camera bay door. There is exhaust discoloration around and aft of the superchargers. (Stan Piet collection)

Photo Variants

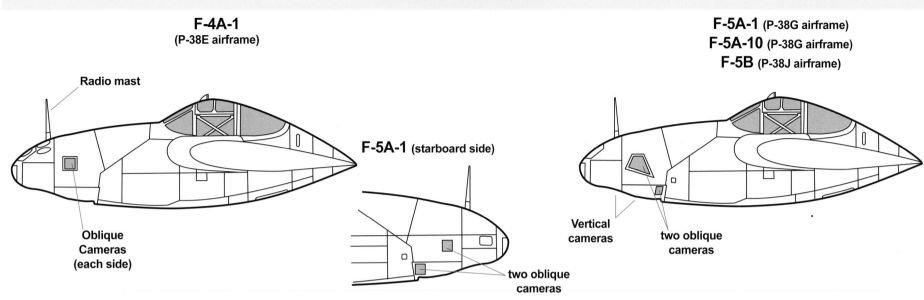

F-4A-1
(P-38E airframe)

Radio mast

Oblique
Cameras
(each side)

F-5A-1 (starboard side)

two oblique
cameras

F-5A-1 (P-38G airframe)
F-5A-10 (P-38G airframe)
F-5B (P-38J airframe)

Vertical
cameras

two oblique
cameras

Because positioning the antenna mast on the underside of the nose of the P-38J would have interfered with the vertical camera's field of view, the mast was relocated to the top of the nose on the F-5B-1-LO. The "kite"-shaped window on the left camera bay door is intended to accommodate an oblique camera. This unusually shaped quadrilateral window featured on the left door only. It appears that the protective contact film on the Plexiglas of that window, while still in place, had started to peel off. It had apparently been overpainted with Synthetic Haze finish. A small number 43 is also painted in yellow on that window. (Stan Piet collection)

Toward the end of World War II, Lockheed increasingly delivered photo-reconnaissance Lightnings with bare-aluminum finishes instead of the Synthetic Haze camouflage schemes. This bare-aluminum F-5E-4-LO, USAAF serial number 44-24225 belonged to the 22nd Photographic Reconnaissance Squadron, 7th Photographic Reconnaissance Group, 325th Reconnaissance Wing, based at USAAF Station 234, Mount Farm, England, from 1944 to 1945. The pilot was Lt. Ellis B. Edwards. The F-5E-4-LO was a conversion of the P-38L-1-LO. Features of this sub-model of the F-5E that distinguished it from the F-5E-2-LO and F-5E-3-LO included a landing light mounted behind Plexiglas on the leading edge of the left wing, and bulged, streamlined fairings for the windows for the oblique cameras on the camera bay doors. Both of these features are visible in this view of technicians loading a camera into the bay. (Stan Piet collection)

F-5E-2-LO, USAAF serial number 43-28616, with the 13th Photographic Reconnaissance Squadron, takes off from Mount Farm, Oxfordshire. This sub-model of the F-5E was a conversion of the P-38J-15-LO. This Lightning was lost on 22 November 1944 and the pilot, Lt. Allan V. Elston, was interned in Sweden. (Stan Piet collection)

The distinctive teardrop-shaped fairing for the window of the oblique camera is visible in this photo of an F-5E painted in a Synthetic Haze camouflage scheme and black and white invasion stripes. These stripes were applied on Allied aircraft at the time of the Normandy Invasion to visually distinguish them from German aircraft, and the stripes often remained on aircraft long after the June 1944 invasion. (Stan Piet collection)

The Florida Gator was an F-5C-1-LO, USAAF serial number 42-67119, with the 22nd Photographic Reconnaissance Squadron, 7th Photographic Reconnaissance Group at Mount Farm, Oxfordshire, England. The F-5C-1-LO model was based on the P-38J-5-LO airframe. *The Florida Gator* was lost on 24 July 1944, and its pilot, Lt. Edward W. Durst, was killed in action. (Stan Piet collection)

Piloted by Lt. R. M. Hairston, *Ginger Snap* was the nickname and the subject of the nose art of this F-5C-1-LO Lightning assigned to the 7th Photographic Reconnaissance Group at RAF Mount Farm, near Dorchester, Oxfordshire, England. The F-5Cs were based on P-38J airframes.

Another photo-reconnaissance Lightning assigned to the 7th Photographic Reconnaissance Group at RAF Mount Farm was this F-5B-1-LO, USAAF serial number 42-68205. The optically flat windows for the cameras were recessed slightly into the sides of the nose. The VHF mast antenna was mounted on top of the nose.

P-38s shipped to Nichols Field on Luzon await reassembly. First in line is an F-5F, a photo-reconnaissance Lightning. The two versions of the F-5F, the F-5F-LO and F-5F-3-LO, were conversions of existing P-38L-5-LOs. The angular chin for the vertical camera windows was the chief identifying feature of the F-5F. (National Archives)

Star Eyes, an F-5B-1-LO with the 28th Photographic Reconnaissance Squadron, boasted markings for 65 photo-recon missions on the side of its central nacelle. Its pilot was a Lt. Howard, and the aircraft was photographed on Ulithi in the Caroline Islands on 28 December 1944. (National Archives)

The P-38L varied only slightly in outward appearance from the P-38J. The retractable landing light was deleted in favor of a fixed landing light behind a Plexiglas cover in the leading edge of the left wing. Booster fuel pumps were installed in the wings, necessitating the addition of two blisters with small access doors under each wing to accommodate the pumps. This example, photographed in the United States, was a P-38L-5-LO. (Stan Piet collection)

The P-38L was the most numerous of the Lightning family, with 3,924 delivered. In addition to the 1,291 P-38L-1-LOs and 2,250 P-38L-5-LOs built by Lockheed's Burbank plant from June 1944 to August 1945, for a total of 3,811, Consolidated Vultee also produced 113 P-38L-5-VNs from January to June 1945 in Nashville, Tennessee. The remainder of the 2,000 Lightnings ordered from Consolidated Vultee were cancelled due to the end of the war.

While externally very similar to the P-38J, inside the aircraft were new engines, the Allison V-1710-111 and -113, each rated at 1,425 horsepower. Also, a gun camera was mounted in an extension at the upper front of the left pylon, a feature that was retrofitted to some earlier Lightnings. The camera was relocated to the pylon because there was less vibration there than in the camera's old location in the nose, near the gun muzzles. Compressibility flaps and additional radio and tail-warning radar antennas were added during production of the P-38L.

No photo reconnaissance versions of the P-38L were factory produced. Rather, the F-5E, F-5F and F-5G aircraft were all converted from completed P-38L aircraft.

Another type converted ex works from the P-38L was the Pathfinder. While the test Pathfinder was converted from a P-38J, all the operational aircraft were modified P-38L aircraft. The Pathfinders were equipped with AN/APS-15 Bombing Through Overcast (BTO) radar in the nose, the operator for which was seated behind the equipment. Whereas most of the base P-38L aircraft were used in the Pacific Theater, the bulk of the Pathfinders operated in the European and Mediterranean Theaters.

New for the Lightnings were the "Christmas tree" rocket launchers, racks holding five 5-inch air-to-ground rockets that were mounted one per wing beginning with the P-38L-5LO, with some being retrofitted to earlier P-38Ls and P-38Js as well.

On a test flight, Lockheed P-38L-5-LO, serial number 44-25419, soars over a sparsely populated area. The aircraft has a low-sheen natural aluminum finish, with matte Olive Drab antiglare panels on the upper inboard parts of the engine nacelles and to the front of the cockpit.

71

Two 1,000-pound bombs are shackled to the pylons of this P-38L-5-LO, serial number 44-25092. Inboard of the pylons, two of the four blisters for the fuel booster pumps are visible. The oval, highly polished surfaces for visually checking the position of the landing gear are visible on the cowlings below and in front of the wings' leading edges.

A P-38L cockpit is viewed from the right side. By now, the prominent gun-charging handle on the lower left of the instrument panel had been deleted. On the left sidewall aft of the throttle quadrant are the rocket control box (top) and the bomb and auxiliary tank release control box (bottom). To the rear of the rocket control box is the radio volume control.

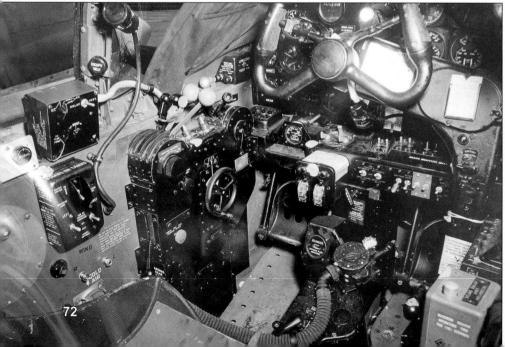

More of the instrument panel is visible in this view of a P-38L cockpit. Like the P-38J, the P-38L had a flat, bulletproof windscreen, eliminating the need for the interior bulletproof glass panel used in earlier models of the Lightning. Above the instrument panel is the L3 reflector sight.

Armorers load the ammunition tray of the right-most machine gun of a late-model P-38 of the 94th Fighter Squadron, 1st Fighter Group, in Italy. On either side of the forearm of the shirtless armorer are the two right spent-casing ejector chutes. (National Archives)

Using manual hoists attached to each side of the pylon and steel cables attached to a cradle under a 1,000-pound bomb, armorers prepare a P-38L-1-LO of the 94th Fighter Squadron for a mission. The man on the left holds the bomb fin. (National Archives)

Two different types of drop tanks have been installed on this P-38L of the 475th Fighter Group at Lingayen Airfield, Luzon, on 25 August 1945: a 165-gallon model on the left pylon and a 310-gallon type for ultra-long distance operations on the right one. Braces are fitted to the 310-gallon tank for stability. (National Archives)

Four P-38Ls, identifiable by the landing lights in the leading edges of their left wings, feature a paint scheme that includes what appear to be natural aluminum and orange markings. Visible are the turbo supercharger intakes and the under-wing bomb/drop tank pylons.

The Lockheed plant at Burbank, California, is shown in an aerial view dated 3 August 1945. According to an inscription on the back of the photo, to the lower center are the three final P-38 Lightnings produced, with the first YP-80 jet fighter to the rear of them.

This droop-snoot Lightning had a different style of clear bombardier's nose than the typical droop snoot, and it lacked the small side windows in the bombardier's compartment. A tilted mast antenna was mounted to the front of the cockpit.

The P-38L Pathfinder conversion had a large radome for an AN/APS-15 BTO (Bombing Through Overcast) radar, behind which was a compartment for the radar operator/bombardier. The Pathfinder led bomb runs in cloudy conditions. This example, seen in Naples, Italy, in April 1945 was converted from a P-38L-1-LO. (Stan Piet collection)

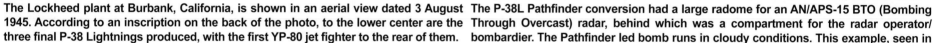

Nose Variants

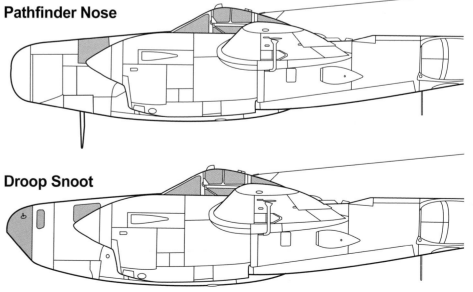

Pathfinder Nose

Droop Snoot

74

P-38L *Hammer's Destruction Co.* assigned to 1st Lt. Samuel E. Hammer, 90th Fighter Squadron, 80th Fighter Group, Tenth Air Force, is parked at an airfield in India. Five Japanese flags signifying aerial kills adorn the fuselage adjacent to the plane's nickname. (National Archives)

Mechanics have rigged a parachute as a sunscreen over a P-38L of the 443rd Fighter Squadron at Lingayen on Luzon, the Philippines, on 29 April 1945. With the cowling panels removed, the left oil coolers of each engine are visible. The landing light in the left wing's leading edge is visible. (National Archives)

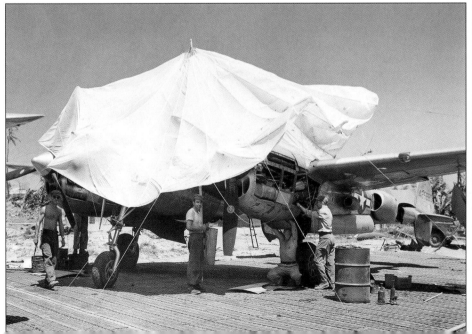

An officer and an enlisted sailor survey the remains of several P-38 Lightnings at a Seventh Air Force base in the Pacific Theater. Even after USAAF aircraft had been written off due to accidents or battle damage, the planes continued to have utility, as they were cannibalized for spare parts to repair or refurbish other P-38s. If undamaged, the guns and engines almost invariably were salvaged. (National Archives)

In order to be able to deploy a night fighter that was faster and nimbler than the larger and heavier P-61 and P-70, the P-38M night fighter was developed. This example, converted from P-38L-5-LO 44-27234, made its first flight in night fighter configuration in July 1944. After being briefly assigned to the 319th Fighter Squadron, where it shown here in flight, it was reassigned to the 418th Night Fighter Squadron in Dobodura, New Guinea, arriving there in August that year. The aircraft was transferred to the 421st Night Fighter Squadron in Fukuoka, Japan, in February 1946, and then flown to Clark Field for scrapping the next month.

The final "production" variant of the Lightning, the P-38M, was in fact not really a production aircraft at all. Rather, the 80 so-called production aircraft were converted from P-38L models at Lockheed's Dallas Modification Center.

These aircraft were the result of an effort to produce a night-fighter that would deliver better performance than the attack bomber-based P-70 or the massive P-61. The prototype P-38M was created by modifying P-83L-5-LO serial number 44-25237.

The conversion included the installation of AN/APS-6 Airborne Intercept (AI) radar housed in a pod that was mounted under the nose, and a compartment for the radar operator, complete with a one-piece Plexiglas canopy. The radar operator's compartment was installed to the rear of the original P-38 cockpit. Following successful testing of the prototype, which process included numerous unsuccessful attempts at creating a shield to protect the pilot's night vision from the glow of the hot turbosupercharger exhaust, a contract was issued. This contract called for 80 P-38L aircraft to be converted to P-38M configuration by Lockheed's Dallas Modification Center.

One prototype and 80 operational P-38Ms were produced, with the first operational aircraft making its maiden flight on 5 January 1945. Production P-38Ms received a gloss black paint finish overall. The P-38 retained all the capabilities of the P-38L, including being equipped with the Christmas tree rocket launchers, despite the roughly 500-pound weight gain caused by the additional crewmen and the modifications to the airframe. Crew training was conducted at Hammer Field, California.

The prototype of the P-38M was converted from a P-38J and was left in bare-aluminum finish. The dark oval on the side of the right engine nacelle is actually the polished metal mirror for visually checking the position of the landing gear.

This P-38M, USAAF serial number 44-26865, was based on a P-38L-5-LO airframe. The name *Night Lightning* is painted on the side of the nose.

The radar operator's quarters in the P-38M were extremely cramped. To his front was the viewing tube for the radar screen, shown here fitted with a cover. A single radio antenna was secured to the rear of the canopy, with the other end attached to the center of the leading edge of the horizontal stabilizer.

P-38M dual cockpit and radome

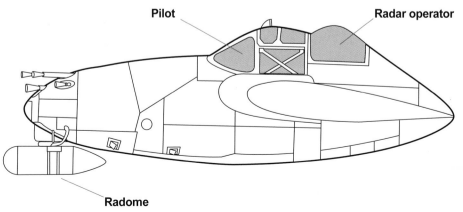

Pilot

Radar operator

Radome

P-38M, USAAF serial number 45-27234, flies over the hills of California. The panels around the turbo-supercharger have been left bare metal. (National Museum of the United States Air Force)

The enlarged canopy of the P-38M is clearly evident on USAAF serial number 44-26865.

P-38M-6-LO serial number 44-27234 was converted to a night-fighter from an airframe originally built as a P-38L-5-LO. This example is equipped with tree launchers for HVARs. The number 7234 is stenciled on the side of the nose. An oval polished-metal panel is on the side of the engine nacelle, to allow the pilot to ascertain the position of the nose landing gear.

Conical flash suppressors were normally fitted to the muzzles of the four .50-caliber machine guns and 20mm cannon so that pilots would not be blinded when firing their guns in the darkness. Sealant is visible around the machine gun barrel where it exits the nose. Markings on the P-38M were in red. (National Archives)

A P-38 Lightning flies over the wing of the F-35 Lightning II on 2 April 2016 during the Luke Air Force Base 2016 air show. The heritage flight features the Air Force's lineage of aircraft from the vintage P-38 to the latest advancement in joint strike fighters, the F-35. (Airman 1st Class Pedro Mota / USAF)